EMMANUEL JOSEPH

Divine Dualities, Integrating Godliness, Romantic Life, Career Goals, and Morality

Copyright © 2025 by Emmanuel Joseph

All rights reserved. No part of this publication may be reproduced, stored or transmitted in any form or by any means, electronic, mechanical, photocopying, recording, scanning, or otherwise without written permission from the publisher. It is illegal to copy this book, post it to a website, or distribute it by any other means without permission.

First edition

This book was professionally typeset on Reedsy.
Find out more at reedsy.com

Contents

1. Chapter 1: The Essence of Duality — 1
2. Chapter 2: The Spiritual Foundation — 3
3. Chapter 3: Love and Relationships — 5
4. Chapter 4: The Pursuit of Career Goals — 7
5. Chapter 5: Ethical Decision-Making — 9
6. Chapter 6: Balancing Dualities — 11
7. Chapter 8: Embracing Imperfection — 13
8. Chapter 9: The Role of Service — 15
9. Chapter 10: Cultivating Gratitude — 17
10. Chapter 11: Embracing Change — 19
11. Chapter 12: Living with Purpose — 21

1

Chapter 1: The Essence of Duality

In the tapestry of life, dualities exist as inherent threads interwoven into our experiences. To understand the essence of duality is to appreciate the balance between opposites, embracing both light and shadow. Dualities can be seen as complementary forces, much like yin and yang, each playing a vital role in the harmony of existence. As we embark on this journey of integrating godliness, romantic life, career goals, and morality, it is essential to recognize that these aspects are not separate compartments but interconnected facets of our being. The challenge lies in navigating these dualities with grace and intentionality.

Life often presents us with seemingly contradictory desires and responsibilities. The quest for spiritual growth may appear at odds with the pursuit of worldly success, while maintaining a fulfilling romantic relationship might feel incompatible with career aspirations. However, embracing duality involves understanding that these aspects can coexist and even enrich one another. By acknowledging and honoring the multifaceted nature of our existence, we can cultivate a holistic approach to living that harmonizes our inner and outer worlds. This chapter lays the foundation for exploring the intricate dance of dualities that shape our lives.

As we delve deeper into the concept of duality, we must also consider the role of personal values and beliefs. Our moral compass serves as a guiding light, helping us navigate the complexities of life. By aligning our actions with our core values, we can create a sense of coherence and integrity amidst the dualities we encounter. This alignment fosters a deeper connection to our true selves and enables us to live with authenticity and purpose. Recognizing the interplay between godliness, romantic life, career goals, and morality is the first step toward integrating these dimensions into a harmonious whole.

The journey of integrating dualities requires a willingness to embrace paradox and ambiguity. It involves letting go of rigid definitions and expectations, allowing for fluidity and adaptability. This openness creates space for growth and transformation, enabling us to evolve in alignment with our higher purpose. By cultivating a mindset of curiosity and acceptance, we can navigate the complexities of life with greater ease and grace. In this chapter, we set the stage for a deeper exploration of the interconnectedness of godliness, romantic life, career goals, and morality.

Ultimately, the essence of duality lies in the recognition that life is a dynamic interplay of opposites. By embracing this interplay, we can transcend the limitations of binary thinking and open ourselves to a more expansive and inclusive understanding of existence. The journey of integrating dualities is not about achieving perfection or eliminating conflict but about finding balance and harmony amidst the complexities of life. As we embark on this exploration, we invite you to embrace the richness and depth of your own unique journey, recognizing that each step is an opportunity for growth and transformation.

2

Chapter 2: The Spiritual Foundation

At the heart of our exploration of dualities lies the concept of godliness, which serves as the spiritual foundation for our journey. Godliness is not confined to religious dogma or rituals but encompasses a deep and abiding connection to the divine essence within and around us. This connection transcends cultural and religious boundaries, inviting us to experience the sacred in everyday life. By cultivating a sense of reverence and gratitude, we can tap into the divine source of wisdom, love, and inspiration that guides our path.

The practice of mindfulness and meditation plays a crucial role in nurturing our spiritual foundation. These practices help us quiet the noise of the external world and tune into the inner voice of our higher self. Through regular meditation, we can develop a deeper awareness of our thoughts, emotions, and intentions, allowing us to align our actions with our spiritual values. Mindfulness invites us to be fully present in each moment, fostering a sense of connection and unity with all that is. This chapter explores various spiritual practices that can help us strengthen our connection to the divine.

In addition to individual practices, community and fellowship are essential components of our spiritual foundation. Engaging with like-minded individuals who share our commitment to spiritual growth can provide support, inspiration, and accountability. By participating in spiritual gatherings, study groups, or service projects, we can deepen our understanding of godliness and its practical application in our lives. The collective energy of a spiritual community can amplify our efforts and create a sense of belonging and purpose.

The integration of godliness into our daily lives involves embodying spiritual principles such as compassion, humility, and integrity. These principles serve as guiding lights, helping us navigate the complexities of our dual existence. By cultivating a compassionate heart, we can extend love and kindness to ourselves and others, fostering a sense of interconnectedness and unity. Humility invites us to recognize our limitations and embrace the wisdom of others, while integrity calls us to live in alignment with our highest values. This chapter delves into the practical application of these principles in our interactions and choices.

Ultimately, the spiritual foundation we cultivate serves as a grounding force amidst the dualities we encounter. It provides a source of strength, resilience, and clarity as we navigate the intricate dance of godliness, romantic life, career goals, and morality. By nurturing our spiritual connection, we can create a sense of inner peace and harmony that permeates every aspect of our lives. This chapter invites you to deepen your relationship with the divine and explore the transformative power of spiritual practices.

3

Chapter 3: Love and Relationships

The journey of integrating dualities extends to the realm of romantic relationships, where love serves as a profound and transformative force. Love is not merely an emotion but a state of being that invites us to connect deeply with another person and experience the divine through the lens of human connection. Romantic relationships provide an opportunity for growth, healing, and self-discovery as we navigate the complexities of intimacy, vulnerability, and commitment. This chapter explores the dynamics of love and relationships, offering insights into creating and sustaining meaningful connections.

At the core of any romantic relationship is the concept of unconditional love, which transcends the limitations of ego and self-interest. Unconditional love invites us to see our partner as a reflection of the divine, worthy of love and acceptance just as they are. This form of love requires a willingness to embrace both the beauty and the imperfections of our partner, recognizing that true connection lies in the authenticity of our shared experiences. By practicing unconditional love, we can create a safe and nurturing space for our relationship to flourish.

Effective communication is a cornerstone of healthy relationships. It involves not only the exchange of words but also the ability to listen deeply and empathetically. By cultivating active listening skills, we can foster a sense of understanding and trust in our relationship. Honest and open communication allows us to express our needs, desires, and boundaries, creating a foundation of mutual respect and partnership. This chapter offers practical strategies for enhancing communication and resolving conflicts in a loving and constructive manner.

The dance of dualities is particularly evident in the balance between individuality and togetherness in a relationship. While it is essential to nurture a deep connection with our partner, it is equally important to honor our own needs and aspirations. Maintaining a sense of individuality allows us to bring our full and authentic selves to the relationship, enriching the partnership with our unique gifts and perspectives. By supporting each other's personal growth and goals, we can create a dynamic and evolving relationship that thrives on mutual support and respect.

The integration of godliness into our romantic life involves recognizing the sacredness of our connection and infusing our relationship with spiritual principles. By cultivating a sense of reverence and gratitude for our partner, we can elevate our relationship to a higher level of spiritual connection. Practices such as shared meditation, prayer, or rituals can help deepen our bond and create a sense of unity and purpose. This chapter invites you to explore the divine dimensions of love and relationships, embracing the transformative power of love as a path to spiritual growth.

4

Chapter 4: The Pursuit of Career Goals

By aligning your career goals with your spiritual values, you can create a sense of purpose and fulfillment that transcends the material aspects of success. This alignment invites you to view your career as a sacred journey, where each challenge and achievement serves as an opportunity for growth and self-discovery. As you navigate the dualities of ambition and contentment, productivity and rest, you can cultivate a deeper understanding of your true purpose and the impact you wish to make in the world.

In the pursuit of career goals, it is essential to recognize the importance of continuous learning and personal development. The ever-evolving nature of the professional landscape requires us to adapt and grow in response to new opportunities and challenges. By committing to lifelong learning, we can stay relevant and competitive while also nurturing our intellectual and spiritual growth. This chapter explores various strategies for ongoing education and skill development, empowering you to thrive in your career while staying true to your higher purpose.

The integration of career goals and spirituality also involves cultivating a sense of gratitude and appreciation for the journey. Gratitude allows us to recognize the blessings and opportunities that come our way, fostering a positive and optimistic outlook. By appreciating the present moment and the progress we have made, we can create a sense of contentment and fulfillment that transcends external measures of success. This chapter invites you to practice gratitude as a powerful tool for enhancing your professional and spiritual well-being.

Ultimately, the pursuit of career goals is a dynamic and evolving journey that requires balance, intentionality, and self-awareness. By aligning your career aspirations with your spiritual values, you can create a sense of harmony and purpose that enriches every aspect of your life. This chapter encourages you to embrace the dualities of career and spirituality, recognizing that your professional journey is an integral part of your broader quest for meaning and fulfillment.

5

Chapter 5: Ethical Decision-Making

The integration of godliness, romantic life, career goals, and morality involves navigating the complex terrain of ethical decision-making. Ethics serves as the moral compass that guides our actions, helping us discern right from wrong and make choices that align with our highest values. By cultivating a strong ethical foundation, we can create a sense of coherence and integrity in our lives, fostering trust and respect in our relationships and professional endeavors. This chapter explores the principles of ethical decision-making and offers practical strategies for navigating moral dilemmas.

At the heart of ethical decision-making is the concept of integrity, which involves living in alignment with our core values and principles. Integrity requires honesty, transparency, and a commitment to doing what is right, even when faced with difficult choices or external pressures. By cultivating integrity, we can create a sense of trust and credibility in our relationships and professional interactions. This chapter delves into the importance of integrity and offers practical guidance on how to cultivate and maintain it in our daily lives.

Ethical decision-making also involves considering the impact of our actions on others and the broader community. This perspective invites us to move beyond self-interest and consider the greater good, recognizing our interconnectedness and the ripple effects of our choices. By adopting a mindset of compassion and empathy, we can make decisions that honor the dignity and well-being of others. This chapter explores various ethical frameworks, such as utilitarianism and deontology, and offers practical strategies for applying these principles in our decision-making process.

The integration of ethics and spirituality involves recognizing the sacredness of our actions and their potential for positive impact. By approaching our decisions with a sense of reverence and mindfulness, we can create a deeper connection to our higher purpose and the divine essence within us. This perspective invites us to see our choices as opportunities for spiritual growth and transformation, fostering a sense of alignment and coherence in our lives. This chapter encourages you to explore the spiritual dimensions of ethical decision-making and embrace the transformative power of living with integrity.

In the realm of career and professional life, ethical decision-making is particularly critical. The dualities of ambition and morality, success and integrity, can create tension and challenge our commitment to ethical principles. By cultivating a strong ethical foundation, we can navigate these dualities with confidence and clarity, making choices that align with our higher values and purpose. This chapter offers practical strategies for maintaining ethical standards in the workplace and addressing ethical dilemmas with integrity and grace.

Ultimately, ethical decision-making is a continuous and evolving process that requires self-awareness, reflection, and a commitment to living in alignment with our highest values. By integrating ethics into every aspect of our lives, we can create a sense of coherence and integrity that enhances our relationships, career, and spiritual well-being. This chapter invites you to embrace the principles of ethical decision-making and explore their transformative potential in your journey of integrating godliness, romantic life, career goals, and morality.

6

Chapter 6: Balancing Dualities

The journey of integrating dualities involves finding a delicate balance between the various aspects of our lives. Balancing dualities is not about achieving perfect equilibrium but about navigating the dynamic interplay of opposites with grace and intentionality. By embracing the fluidity and complexity of life, we can create a sense of harmony and well-being that transcends rigid definitions and expectations. This chapter explores the art of balancing dualities and offers practical strategies for cultivating a holistic and integrated approach to living.

At the core of balancing dualities is the concept of mindfulness, which involves being fully present and aware of our thoughts, emotions, and actions. Mindfulness invites us to approach life with curiosity and acceptance, allowing us to navigate the complexities of dual existence with greater ease and grace. By cultivating mindfulness, we can create a sense of inner peace and balance that permeates every aspect of our lives. This chapter offers practical guidance on mindfulness practices, such as meditation and mindful breathing, and their application in daily life.

The balance between godliness and worldly pursuits is a common duality that many of us encounter. By recognizing that spiritual growth and material success are not mutually exclusive, we can create a sense of harmony and fulfillment. This perspective invites us to see our worldly pursuits as opportunities for spiritual expression and growth, fostering a deeper connection to our higher purpose. This chapter explores various strategies for integrating spirituality into our daily activities and finding balance between our inner and outer worlds.

Balancing dualities also involves honoring our unique rhythms and needs. Each of us has different strengths, preferences, and limitations, and it is essential to recognize and honor these individual differences. By listening to our bodies and intuition, we can create a sense of balance that is authentic and sustainable. This chapter offers practical strategies for self-care, time management, and boundary setting, empowering you to navigate the demands of life with resilience and grace.

The integration of dualities requires a willingness to embrace paradox and ambiguity. Life is not always black and white, and the ability to hold multiple perspectives simultaneously can create a sense of depth and richness in our experiences. By cultivating a mindset of openness and adaptability, we can navigate the complexities of dual existence with greater ease and flexibility. This chapter encourages you to explore the art of balancing dualities and embrace the transformative potential of living with intention and awareness.

Ultimately, balancing dualities is an ongoing and dynamic process that requires self-awareness, reflection, and intentionality. By embracing the fluidity and complexity of life, we can create a sense of harmony and well-being that transcends rigid definitions and expectations. This chapter invites you to explore the art of balancing dualities and cultivate a holistic and integrated approach to living, recognizing that each moment is an opportunity for growth and transformation.

7

Chapter 8: Embracing Imperfection

The journey of integrating dualities involves embracing imperfection as an inherent and valuable aspect of our existence. Perfection is an elusive and often unattainable ideal that can create a sense of pressure and inadequacy. By recognizing that imperfection is a natural part of the human experience, we can cultivate a sense of acceptance and compassion for ourselves and others. This chapter explores the concept of embracing imperfection and offers practical strategies for cultivating self-compassion and resilience.

At the heart of embracing imperfection is the concept of self-compassion, which involves treating ourselves with kindness and understanding, especially in moments of struggle or failure. Self-compassion invites us to acknowledge our imperfections and vulnerabilities without judgment, recognizing that they are part of what makes us human. By practicing self-compassion, we can create a sense of inner peace and resilience that empowers us to navigate the complexities of life with greater ease and grace. This chapter offers practical guidance on self-compassion practices, such as self-reflection, mindfulness, and self-care.

The integration of imperfection and godliness involves recognizing that our spiritual journey is a continuous and evolving process. Spiritual growth is not about achieving a state of perfection but about embracing the journey with curiosity and openness. By acknowledging our imperfections and seeking growth and transformation, we can deepen our connection to the divine and our higher purpose. This chapter explores various spiritual practices that support the acceptance of imperfection, such as prayer, meditation, and journaling.

In the realm of romantic relationships, embracing imperfection involves recognizing that both we and our partners are imperfect beings. By approaching our relationships with a sense of acceptance and compassion, we can create a safe and nurturing space for growth and connection. This perspective invites us to see our partner's imperfections as opportunities for deepening our understanding and love. This chapter offers practical strategies for fostering acceptance and compassion in our relationships, enhancing communication, and resolving conflicts with empathy and grace.

The integration of imperfection and career involves recognizing that professional success is not defined by the absence of mistakes or failures but by the ability to learn and grow from them. By embracing a growth mindset, we can view challenges and setbacks as opportunities for development and innovation. This chapter encourages you to approach your career with a sense of curiosity and resilience, recognizing that imperfection is a natural part of the professional journey. Practical strategies for cultivating a growth mindset, learning from failures, and embracing continuous improvement are explored in this chapter.

Ultimately, embracing imperfection is a transformative practice that empowers us to live with authenticity, compassion, and resilience. By accepting our imperfections and those of others, we can create a sense of connection and unity that transcends the limitations of perfectionism. This chapter invites you to explore the concept of embracing imperfection and cultivate a mindset of acceptance and self-compassion on your journey of integrating godliness, romantic life, career goals, and morality.

8

Chapter 9: The Role of Service

The journey of integrating dualities involves recognizing the transformative power of service, which connects us to the broader community and fosters a sense of purpose and fulfillment. Service is an expression of our higher values and a pathway to contribute to the greater good. By engaging in acts of service, we can create a positive impact on the world and deepen our connection to the divine essence within and around us. This chapter explores the role of service in our lives and offers practical strategies for integrating service into our daily routines.

At the heart of service is the concept of compassion, which involves extending love and kindness to others and recognizing our interconnectedness. Compassion invites us to see the divine in every individual and to approach our interactions with empathy and understanding. By cultivating a compassionate heart, we can create a sense of unity and purpose in our lives. This chapter explores various practices for cultivating compassion, such as volunteer work, random acts of kindness, and mindfulness exercises.

The integration of service and godliness involves recognizing that service is a sacred expression of our spiritual values. By approaching acts of service with a sense of reverence and gratitude, we can deepen our connection to the divine and our higher purpose. This perspective invites us to see service as an opportunity for spiritual growth and transformation, fostering a deeper sense of fulfillment and meaning. This chapter offers practical strategies for incorporating service into our spiritual practices and daily routines.

In the realm of romantic relationships, the role of service involves recognizing the importance of supporting and uplifting our partners. By approaching our relationships with a spirit of service, we can create a sense of mutual respect and partnership. This perspective invites us to be attentive to our partner's needs and to offer our support and love in meaningful ways. This chapter explores various strategies for integrating service into our relationships, enhancing communication, and fostering a sense of connection and intimacy.

The integration of service and career involves recognizing that our professional endeavors can be a powerful platform for positive impact. By aligning our career goals with a sense of service, we can create a sense of purpose and fulfillment in our work. This chapter encourages you to explore ways to incorporate service into your professional life, such as mentoring, pro bono work, or community engagement. Practical strategies for balancing service and career aspirations are also explored in this chapter.

Ultimately, the role of service is a transformative practice that empowers us to live with purpose, compassion, and alignment. By engaging in acts of service, we can create a positive impact on the world and deepen our connection to the divine essence within and around us. This chapter invites you to explore the transformative power of service and integrate it into your journey of integrating godliness, romantic life, career goals, and morality.

9

Chapter 10: Cultivating Gratitude

The journey of integrating dualities involves cultivating gratitude as a powerful tool for enhancing our well-being and fostering a sense of fulfillment. Gratitude is the practice of recognizing and appreciating the blessings and opportunities in our lives, fostering a positive and optimistic outlook. By cultivating gratitude, we can create a sense of contentment and joy that transcends external circumstances. This chapter explores the concept of gratitude and offers practical strategies for incorporating gratitude into our daily routines.

At the heart of gratitude is the concept of appreciation, which involves recognizing the value and beauty in our experiences, relationships, and surroundings. Appreciation invites us to be fully present and attentive to the richness of life, fostering a sense of wonder and awe. By practicing appreciation, we can create a deeper connection to the present moment and enhance our overall well-being. This chapter explores various practices for cultivating appreciation, such as gratitude journaling, mindful breathing, and nature walks.

The integration of gratitude and career involves recognizing the opportunities and growth experiences in our professional journey. By approaching our career with a sense of gratitude, we can create a positive and optimistic outlook that enhances our motivation and resilience. This chapter encourages you to practice gratitude in your professional life, recognizing the value and impact of your work, and appreciating the support and contributions of colleagues and mentors. Practical strategies for cultivating gratitude in the workplace, such as expressing appreciation, acknowledging achievements, and fostering a positive work environment, are explored in this chapter.

Ultimately, cultivating gratitude is a transformative practice that empowers us to live with a sense of contentment, joy, and fulfillment. By recognizing and appreciating the blessings and opportunities in our lives, we can create a positive and optimistic outlook that transcends external circumstances. This chapter invites you to explore the transformative power of gratitude and integrate it into your journey of integrating godliness, romantic life, career goals, and morality.

10

Chapter 11: Embracing Change

The journey of integrating dualities involves embracing change as a natural and inevitable aspect of life. Change is a constant and dynamic force that shapes our experiences, relationships, and aspirations. By embracing change with openness and adaptability, we can navigate the complexities of life with greater ease and resilience. This chapter explores the concept of embracing change and offers practical strategies for cultivating a mindset of flexibility and growth.

At the heart of embracing change is the concept of adaptability, which involves the ability to adjust and respond to new circumstances and opportunities. Adaptability requires a willingness to let go of rigid definitions and expectations, allowing for fluidity and transformation. By cultivating a mindset of adaptability, we can create a sense of resilience and resourcefulness that empowers us to navigate the uncertainties of life. This chapter offers practical guidance on adaptability practices, such as mindfulness, reflection, and goal-setting.

The integration of change and godliness involves recognizing that spiritual growth is a continuous and evolving process. By embracing change as an opportunity for spiritual transformation, we can deepen our connection to the divine and our higher purpose. This perspective invites us to see change as a sacred journey of growth and discovery, fostering a deeper sense of alignment and fulfillment. This chapter explores various spiritual practices that support the acceptance of change, such as meditation, prayer, and journaling.

In the realm of romantic relationships, embracing change involves recognizing that both we and our partners are continuously evolving beings. By approaching our relationships with a sense of openness and adaptability, we can create a dynamic and evolving connection that thrives on mutual growth and transformation. This perspective invites us to embrace the changes and transitions in our relationship as opportunities for deepening our understanding and love. This chapter explores various strategies for navigating change in relationships, enhancing communication, and fostering a sense of connection and intimacy.

The integration of change and career involves recognizing that professional growth and advancement are dynamic and evolving processes. By embracing change as an opportunity for innovation and development, we can create a sense of excitement and motivation in our work. This chapter encourages you to approach your career with a mindset of flexibility and curiosity, recognizing that change is a natural part of the professional journey. Practical strategies for navigating career transitions, adapting to new roles, and embracing continuous learning are explored in this chapter.

Ultimately, embracing change is a transformative practice that empowers us to live with resilience, adaptability, and openness. By recognizing that change is a natural and inevitable aspect of life, we can create a sense of ease and flexibility that transcends the limitations of rigidity and resistance. This chapter invites you to explore the concept of embracing change and cultivate a mindset of adaptability and growth on your journey of integrating godliness, romantic life, career goals, and morality.

11

Chapter 12: Living with Purpose

The culmination of our journey of integrating dualities involves living with purpose, which serves as the guiding force that shapes our actions, relationships, and aspirations. Purpose is the conscious choice to align our lives with our higher values and aspirations, creating a sense of meaning and fulfillment. By living with purpose, we can navigate the complexities of life with confidence, clarity, and intentionality. This chapter explores the concept of living with purpose and offers practical strategies for cultivating a purposeful and fulfilling life.

At the heart of living with purpose is the concept of alignment, which involves living in harmony with our true selves and higher purpose. Alignment requires self-awareness, reflection, and a commitment to living with authenticity and integrity. By aligning our actions with our values and aspirations, we can create a sense of coherence and purpose that permeates every aspect of our lives. This chapter offers practical guidance on the process of alignment, including self-reflection exercises, goal-setting, and action planning.

The integration of purpose and godliness involves recognizing that our higher purpose is a reflection of the divine essence within us. By approaching our purpose with a sense of reverence and gratitude, we can deepen our connection to the divine and our higher purpose. This perspective invites us to see our purpose as a sacred journey of growth and transformation, fostering a deeper sense of fulfillment and meaning. This chapter explores various spiritual practices that support the cultivation of purpose, such as meditation, prayer, and journaling.

In the realm of romantic relationships, living with purpose involves recognizing that our relationships can be a powerful expression of our higher values and aspirations. By approaching our relationships with intentionality and purpose, we can create a sense of alignment and fulfillment that enhances our connection with our partner. This perspective invites us to set relationship goals and intentions that reflect our higher purpose, fostering a sense of mutual growth and partnership. This chapter explores various strategies for cultivating purpose in our relationships, enhancing communication, and deepening our connection and intimacy.

The integration of purpose and career involves recognizing that our professional endeavors can be a powerful platform for expressing our higher values and aspirations. By aligning our career goals with our higher purpose, we can create a sense of fulfillment and meaning in our work. This chapter encourages you to approach your career with a sense of purpose and intentionality, recognizing that your professional journey is an integral part of your broader quest for meaning and fulfillment. Practical strategies for setting career goals, developing action plans, and aligning your work with your higher purpose are explored in this chapter.

Ultimately, living with purpose is a transformative practice that empowers us to live with confidence, clarity, and intentionality. By aligning our lives with our higher values and aspirations, we can create a sense of meaning and fulfillment that transcends the complexities of life. This chapter invites you to explore the concept of living with purpose and cultivate a purposeful and fulfilling life on your journey of integrating godliness, romantic life, career goals, and morality.

Book Description for "Divine Dualities: Integrating Godliness, Romantic Life, Career Goals, and Morality"

In "Divine Dualities: Integrating Godliness, Romantic Life, Career Goals, and Morality," embark on a transformative journey to harmonize the multifaceted dimensions of your existence. This thought-provoking book

CHAPTER 12: LIVING WITH PURPOSE

delves into the intricate dance between spirituality, love, professional aspirations, and ethical living, offering a holistic approach to leading a fulfilling and purpose-driven life.

Explore the essence of duality and uncover the profound interconnectedness of these seemingly contradictory aspects. Learn to cultivate a strong spiritual foundation that guides your path, infusing your daily life with mindfulness, meditation, and a sense of reverence. Discover the dynamics of love and relationships, where unconditional love, effective communication, and shared spiritual practices foster deep and meaningful connections.

Navigate the pursuit of career goals with intentionality and alignment, recognizing the sacred potential of your professional endeavors. Balance ambition with ethical decision-making, fostering integrity and compassion in your actions. Embrace imperfection and resilience, recognizing that growth and self-discovery are continuous journeys.

Through the power of intention, embrace change with adaptability and openness, transforming challenges into opportunities for personal and spiritual growth. Cultivate gratitude and service, fostering a sense of contentment, joy, and positive impact on the world. Ultimately, live with purpose, aligning your life with your highest values and aspirations, and creating a sense of coherence and fulfillment.

"Divine Dualities" is a compelling guide for anyone seeking to integrate godliness, romantic life, career goals, and morality into a harmonious and enriching existence. With practical strategies, insightful reflections, and spiritual wisdom, this book invites you to embark on a journey of growth, transformation, and intentional living.

www.ingramcontent.com/pod-product-compliance
Lightning Source LLC
LaVergne TN
LVHW020508080526
838202LV00057B/6234